Trapped in Paradise

by Jeremy D. Hooper

Trapped in Paradise

Library of Congress Control Number: 2024901343

Printed in the United States of America

Publisher's Cataloging-in-Publication data

Names: Hooper, Jeremy D., author.
Title: Trapped in paradise / Jeremy D. Hooper.
Description: San Antonio, TX: Jeremy Hooper, 2024.
Identifiers: LCCN: 2024901343 | ISBN: 979-8-218-28608-8
Subjects: LCSH Hooper, Jeremy D.--Travel--Hawaii. | Natural disasters--Hawaii. | Maui (Hawaii)--Description and travel. | BISAC BIOGRAPHY & AUTOBIOGRAPHY / Memoirs | BIOGRAPHY & AUTOBIOGRAPHY / Survival
Classification: LCC DU628.M3 .H66 2024 | DDC 919.69--dc23

This is the story of two Hawaiian vacationers who found themselves in midst of unspeakable devastation on Maui in August 2023 when deadly wildfires destroyed much of the west side of the island. This book is dedicated to the courageous people of Lahaina who will rebuild their iconic and historic town that lies in one of the most beautiful places on earth.

Chapter 1

MY FAVORITE TRAVEL companion is my 20-year-old second cousin Kaidyn. Having just completed two years at San Antonio College, she had a few weeks of summer break before she begins her studies at the University of Texas at San Antonio in the fall. Our last trip was to New York City in March. I took her to see the Museum of Natural History, the Wax Museum in Times Square, the Empire State Building, the World Trade Center, the Statue of Liberty, and a few other landmarks. The highlight of the trip was seeing Disney's *The Lion King* on Broadway. While I believe that Kaidyn enjoyed the trip, the hustle and bustle of city life might have been a little overwhelming for her. Travel delays and the constant moving from one event to the next was not what I think this college girl needed. I felt like she was looking for a place to relax at an oceanfront resort and just get away from it all. What better place for this than Maui?

Kaidyn reached out on July 15th and asked me what my schedule was like in August. She expressed interest in taking a trip since her classes would be over: "I was thinking a cruise maybe or Hawaii.". I told her that I didn't have a solid schedule for August yet but would let her know when I did. My work as a captain for a major airline and officer in the U.S. Air Force reserve places significant demands on my availability, but there is also a healthy amount of flexibility to make adjustments. I was trying to fly a mission for the Air Force in August so that we could complete the aircraft commander upgrade process for one of our squadron's pilots. As one of the few C-5M evaluator pilots who was not medically grounded or otherwise unavailable, I was needed to administer the check ride to this particular pilot. Due to constant schedule changes and mission cancellations, it was difficult to predict when I would be able to make myself available for a little unscheduled vacation.

In the ensuing days, it appeared that we had firmed up the dates for the military trip—it would be August 14-20. I also had a Unit Training Assembly (UTA) (a.k.a. "drill weekend") on August 5-6 and an airline trip on August 11-12. I would need to get rid of the airline trip in order to make a personal adventure to the Hawaiian

Islands worth the effort. Dropping that rotation wasn't the easiest task. Another pilot would have to voluntarily pick the trip up from me, or there would have to be sufficient coverage of reserve pilots that the company could task with the rotation. Neither of these are likely scenarios during a weekend in the middle of the busy summer travel season. Fortunately, I was able to move a vacation day from later on in the year and use it to force the unwanted airline trip from my schedule. Once I had cleared the week of significant obligations, I was ready to commit to this island expedition.

Kaidyn informed me that she wanted to go to Hawaii, so I told her to look at the different islands and decide where she wanted to visit: Oahu, Maui, Kauai, or the big island. They are all entirely different places with their own plusses and minuses, I said. She texted me back on July 20th and said she wanted to go to the big island or to Maui. I responded that there would likely be more of interest to do in Maui and asked if she was serious about going on the trip. I didn't want to mess with standby travel on my airline benefits, so I knew that once I started booking tickets and hotel rooms that I probably wasn't going to get my money back if we decided not to take the trip. She told me she was serious and had already coordinated for time off work.

I decided for this trip that I was going to spare few expenses, and we were going to travel in style. We'd have confirmed first class tickets on a widebody airplane with the lie-flat seats, and I was going to book rooms at a resort hotel with a nice swimming pool, spa services, and direct access to the beach. I let Kaidyn book whatever activities she wanted, which included a dinner cruise, a massage, and snorkeling at Molokini. The only thing I said "no" to was a private tour guide to drive us to Hana for approximately $1,400. I told her we could drive ourselves to Hana and make all the stops along the way—without a tour guide. For certain, I could have planned the trip much more economically, but I had done quite well working in July—earning an above average amount in paystubs. Coupled with the realization that Kaidyn has now grown up and the window of opportunity to take these kinds of trips with her may be dwindling to a close in the coming years—I figured we could afford it. You only live once, right?

I shopped all the major U.S. airlines offering widebody service to Hawaii (American, Delta, Hawaiian, and United) and settled on an itinerary from United Airlines, departing at 6:45am on Monday, August 7. It was not the most convenient routing as we would have to fly from San Antonio to Chicago and then to Kahului, Maui. On the way back, we were ticketed to fly from Kahului to San Francisco on the redeye flight leaving on Friday, August 11 and then to Houston before the final leg to San Antonio. We would be in Polaris / First Class for the entire trip, flying on a Boeing 787

Dreamliner from Chicago to Maui and then to San Francisco on a Boeing 777 in lie flat seats, all for a reasonable price. I considered booking a nonstop flight from Austin to Honolulu on the Hawaiian Airlines A330 service that operates every other day, but we would have had to drive to Austin and still board a connecting flight from Oahu to Maui—and besides (this is key), only economy class seats were available on the return flight.

When searching for hotel accommodations, I typically look on Hotwire for any good deals. One drawback of Hotwire is that you may not know where you are staying until you have a nonrefundable "reservation" (you'll see why I used air quotes later on in the story). I also reached out to my friend Lori who recently traveled to the island and has a knack for finding bargains. She suggested some properties, including the Marriott Ocean Club that sits three miles north of Lahaina. My basic criteria were that it had to sit directly on the beach and have that "resort" atmosphere associated with being in paradise. Ideally, we would have our own rooms or a suite with a separate bedroom so that we could be afforded an appropriate level of privacy. This wasn't the absolute nicest resort on Maui, but it fit the bill with large villas and a full kitchen, living room, and private bedroom with jacuzzi tub and a walk-in shower. The price was within the realm of reason at approx. $1,000/room/night, which was on par with what a 'regular' room cost at nearby properties. I booked us four nights at the Marriott Ocean Club.

In the early morning hours on August 1, after returning to San Antonio from Atlanta for a FAA physical exam, I received a phone call from the Memorial Herman Medical Center in The Woodlands, Texas. My sister Niki had been involved in a vehicle-pedestrian accident and was going to be undergoing surgery. Up to this point I was concerned that she might lose her leg or worse, but Dr. Smith called me at 2:18am when the surgery was over and informed me that everything had gone well. She had been walking near her home with her 10-year-old son when a hit-and-run pickup truck struck her with the vehicle and left her for dead. Fortunately, her son was able to run for help and call for the paramedics.

I called both of my parents who were vacationing in different cities. My mom and stepdad were in their RV returning from Colorado while my dad and stepmom were visiting my aunt in Tennessee. Neither parent answered their phone due to the late hour, but I was able to relay the message through my aunt to my dad. Niki lives with her son and former coworker Ruth, so she had some local support. However, I was the closest family member to the hospital and decided to drive to Houston to see her later that afternoon. I visited her hospital room twice, both before and after her second surgery. She was not in the best shape and still faces a long road to recovery, but my mom was returning to town on August 4 and would be able to better tend to her needs. Able to do little more, I returned to San Antonio for my drill weekend and determined that I could proceed to Maui with little consequence.

UTA weekends are a mixed bag. While it can be a small pain to sit through boring briefings and administrivia, it is usually fun to catch up with the guys. Around lunch time, the chief pilot sent out a group text message looking for a pilot to jump on the local flight that was carrying the wing's civilian employers (a.k.a. Boss Lift) on a tour of south-central Texas. My buddy Ross was the Instructor Pilot (IP) so I was happy to be able to fly with him. With passengers on board, we couldn't perform touch-and-go landings so I didn't get to do any of the flying myself, but I was able to sit in the right seat and help one of my peers regain his flying currency and administer a "no notice" check ride to the new lieutenant who was flying with us.

That evening, we had a pilot social event at a local brewery. I don't drink anymore, but if you're not willing to hang out at a place that serves alcohol every once in a while, you won't be hanging out with too many of (these) pilots. It seemed like there was less to do on Sunday except 'death by PowerPoint' briefings, but it was a productive weekend. At the conclusion of the UTA, I drove out of the gate in anticipation for the week in Maui, effectively brain dumping everything work-related from my list of concerns.

Chapter 2

THE FLIGHT TO Chicago left at 6:45am, so I knew we needed to be at the airport early. While I can always get through TSA screening very quickly as an airline crewmember, the same is not true for Kaidyn. She did not sign up for TSA Precheck, Global Entry, or Clear; therefore, she qualifies for 'standard' screening. This means that she gets to stand in the longest available line for security. Lines can get very long on Monday morning at that hour, and the last thing we wanted to do was miss our flight—and therefore miss our 787 Dreamliner to Maui. I told Kaidyn that I would pick her up at 4:45am. I ensured my two cats and three kittens had enough food, water, and clean litter boxes to last until we were to return on Saturday. I packed my bag with a swimsuit, sunglasses, hat, sunscreen, and my DJI Avata camera drone—all the essentials. According to my Garmin watch that tracks my sleep, I awoke at 2:20am and picked Kaidyn up at her Nana's house on time to drive to the San Antonio International Airport.

In contrast to our New York trip where we had to scramble to find parking, spots were readily available in the short-term parking garage so it was a short walk to the terminal. Check-in lines were also thin so we both checked our suitcases. Even the TSA line was less than five minutes long. By the time we cleared security, we had over an hour before we needed to board our flight. Lori had told me that the United Club would let military members in for free so we stopped by. The lady behind the counter was nice and asked if we were on vacation. I told her "yes", but for some reason, she still wanted to see my "orders"—which I had none to show her. She told me to bring them next time but that we could come in anyway. The club offered cereal, pastries, juices, coffee, cappuccino, and a place to relax away from the chaos.

Soon it was time to board our flight to Chicago. One perk of being in the military is the privilege of pre-boarding, so we were among the first to board the Airbus 319 and took our seats in 2E and 2F. The flight attendant Lynette was a little gruff, barking orders at fellow passengers to keep the overhead bin with all the emergency equipment closed. When she came to take my breakfast order, she called me by the wrong name. When I told her that my name is Jeremy, she looked over at seats 2A and 2B where the customer she was looking for was sitting. She jumped around the cabin taking breakfast orders, presumably in order of status on United Airlines. Since we had none, there was no longer a choice of menu items by the time she got back to Kaidyn and me. Not a huge deal, I thought, as I'm not much of a breakfast person anyway. The captain came into the cabin to introduce himself and gave a short spiel. Kaidyn asked me if I do the same when I'm flying. I told her 'good on this guy' for doing that but that I usually stayed in the cockpit when passengers are boarding. Once I knew we were really on our way to Hawaii, I told Kaidyn she could start booking activities. She reserved us a dinner cruise and a snorkeling tour, but the horseback riding was sold out. We both slept most of the way to Chicago due to the lack of sleep the night before, but soon we were on the ground at O'Hare.

It was a pretty short walk to our next gate, and we had an hour or so to kill before we would board our Boeing 787 Dreamliner headed for Maui. I asked Kaidyn if she wanted to find another lounge to hang out in, but she seemed okay to just head to the gate. Like most young people these days, her smartphone provided the needed entertainment to pass the time. Our aircraft was using two jet bridges to board, one for first class and one for economy class. When military members were invited to board, we proceeded towards the jetway being used to board first class. After stepping into the cabin, we made the right turn down the port side of the airplane. We were both seated in window seats that were each situated by themselves with direct aisle access. I was in 5A and Kaidyn was in 6A, and our seats were separated by a galley area adjacent to the #2 left boarding door. I told her that she could take my seat if she wanted it or her own--that it didn't matter to me. Initially, she said she would take my seat so I went back to 6A. Noticing that 6A had a bit of a better window view and was located in a smaller, more private cabin area, I told Kaidyn that she should compare the two and decide where she wanted to sit for the next nine hours. She decided to go ahead and take her original seat, so I returned to 5A. We pushed back from the gate about seven minutes late and taxied out to runway 9C. About 15 minutes later, the General Electric GEnx turbofan engines spooled to life and we gracefully lifted into the sky and were on our way to paradise.

As soon as possible after takeoff, I turned my seat into a lie-flat bed and went to sleep for most of the way across the continental United States—skipping lunch. My blanket that was sitting on the ledge behind my seat had disappeared, but I was tired enough that it didn't matter. When we were well off the coast of California, I watched a couple of documentaries including a 2015 film called *Living in the Age of Airplanes* and another one about Air Force One. I checked on Kaidyn a couple of times. The first time she was still sleeping with the shoulder harness on that they make you wear for takeoff and landing. I unclipped the shoulder harness so she could rest more comfortably. The second time she seemed to be doing well, keeping herself occupied. After reading a few chapters from the textbook for my master's degree class, I treated myself to a burger and coke. Soon, we were on our descent into Kahului.

The airport sits in the valley between two mountains on the east and west side of the island. A pilot announced on the public address system that the winds were gusting up to 35 miles per hour, so it would likely be turbulent on our way down. This is fairly typical for this environment where mountainous terrain and high winds are always a recipe for bumpy air. Runway 02 itself is a relatively short 6,998 feet long, so I knew that after the pilot added additional airspeed on approach to compensate for the windy conditions that the airplane would be coming to an abrupt stop after touchdown. My expectations were not disappointed. After landing, my cell phone that had been sitting on the table leaped to the front of the cabin and a flight attendant had to return it to me when we cleared the runway.

We deplaned uneventfully and proceeded to baggage claim. It seemed to take a long time, perhaps 30 minutes, to retrieve our luggage. Then, we were off to the rental car center via a short train ride. I reserved a car with Hertz; as a gold status member the process is normally seamless, and I can avoid standing in lines. However, today the agent told me that they were behind on washing the cars so it might take another 40 minutes before our car was ready. I told him that it wouldn't hurt my feelings if they skipped running my car through the wash, but he said they would get in trouble for that. We really only waited about 20 minutes before they called my name. I was handed the keys and directed to a nearby parking spot, and soon we were on our way to the Marriott Ocean Club on the west side.

Chapter 3

THERE ARE TWO roads that lead to Lahaina. The main road takes you south from the airport to the coastline and on a clockwise fashion around the Pu'u Kukai peak and the West Maui Forest Reserve. I figured we would take that road later on our way to the dinner cruise that meets near Kihei. For the drive to the resort, we would take the 'scenic' route along a winding road that hugs the cliffs on the northwest side of the island through Kahakuloa. Several areas of the road narrow to a single lane, and it is sometimes necessary to stop so that opposite-direction traffic can proceed across a bridge or a narrow stretch of roadway. Cell phone service is generally unavailable. It is a decidedly more hazardous drive, but I have done it a few times before and appreciated the level of caution the road requires. After taking this route once, the plan was to use the main Honoapiilani Highway to transition between the resort and the rest of the island for the duration of the trip.

The views are, as they say, to 'die' for. Otherwise, what is the point of taking the more dangerous route? I didn't have a death wish, but a seasoned driver who takes it slowly and carefully can complete the task safely. I thoroughly enjoyed the drive, and while Kaidyn had connected her phone to the car's entertainment system via Bluetooth to listen to her tunes—she slept for much of the way. Near Mokolea Point between Kahakuloa and Kapalua, the road develops a normal two-lane flavor, although there are still many twists and turns in the road that demand the driver's full attention. At some point, I made a wrong turn toward a set of resort hotels near Kapalua. It was a short detour that took us next to a grocery store and a number of other places that we could have stocked up on food and essentials. One of my biggest regrets from the trip is not making that stop; after all, our hotel room was equipped with a full kitchen and large refrigerator/freezer. After a full day of travel, we just wanted to get checked into our hotel, and of course we would have a nice dinner on the beach at one of the resort restaurants. I knew I should have brought my mom on the trip. She would have demanded a grocery store stop on the way into town, but who knew of the crisis to come?

While I had the hotel's address plugged into my phone's GPS, for some reason it did not alert me of the right turn we were supposed to make onto Kaanapali Parkway. While Kaidyn still slept, I was already in Lahaina before I realized that I had missed the turn toward the hotel. I made a U-turn on Honoapiilani Highway near Kapunakea Street and proceeded northbound back to Kaanapali Parkway. Sadly, nearly every one of the hundreds of homes, buildings, and structures that we passed between Kapunakea Street and Leialii Parkway would be reduced to a pile of rubble by Wednesday.

We pulled into what looked like a valet parking area near the hotel check-in area. I found a place where it looked okay to stop for a few minutes, and then Kaidyn and I grabbed our suitcases so that we could check in to the hotel. The clerk informed us that we were staying in the Lahaina tower and that it would be easier to drive ourselves to the adjacent parking garage. We found our room #5201 on the 5th floor. It was as advertised with a full kitchen, a living room area for me, a private bedroom area for Kaidyn, a jacuzzi tub, and a walk-in shower. There was a balcony that overlooked the ocean and even a washer/dryer combination. These were the types of villas that are used by timeshare owners, but they are rented out like normal hotel rooms when they are not being used. It would be the perfect place to enjoy four nights on the Island of Maui.

As sunset was near, we wasted no time in checking out the beach. Situated in front of the resort, the beach had a private feel to it—nowhere near as crowded as, say, Waikiki Beach. The sanded area was a fairly narrow strip, but the coastline was long enough to enjoy a stroll past several other resort properties that lied on either side of the Marriott, including the Hyatt Regency and the Westin. The nearby islands of Lana'i and Moloka'i were in view to our west. We walked north on the beach toward the setting sun, played in the water a little, and then walked back toward our hotel for dinner.

If there was one 'normal' night of this vacation, it was the Monday immediately after we arrived. We sat down outside at the well-occupied Longhi's restaurant that served mostly Italian food. The nice waitress ran us through the cocktail menu. Of course, we don't drink so I ordered a sparkling water and Kaidyn ordered a virgin edition of one of the offered drinks. She explained the evening special as a delicious ravioli. My mouth watered as she described this dish, so we both ordered it. It was every bit as delicious as she described. While we were tempted for dessert, we told her that we were full and would return tomorrow to try the chocolate cake and ice cream. I don't remember the nice lady's name, but I do wonder what happened to the waitress and her family.

Chapter 4

THE NEXT MORNING, we woke up around 7:00am. My body clock always seems to be on Hawaii time which is the only place that I like to get up at a 'normal' time. The power was out, but I didn't think much of it. I figured that it would be restored within a few hours. Besides, who cares anyway? We would be enjoying the beach and Pacific Ocean outside, so who needs electricity for that? I learned that the pools were closed as a result; a minor inconvenience as I did want to experience the very nice pool that they have at the Marriott. Kaidyn wanted to go to the Starbucks where a limited selection was available and only room charges were being accepted. We found a cabana on the waterfront with a view of Lana'i so that we could relax and just appreciate the ocean views. After all, that was the point as we weren't looking to necessarily bounce from one activity to the next like we were in New York.

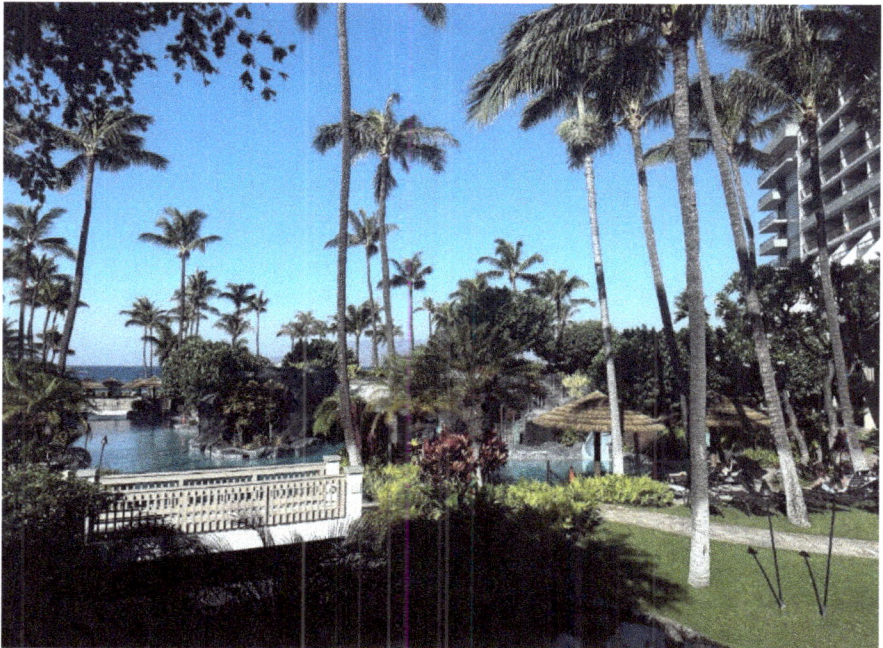

Eventually, a hotel employee informed us that the cabana we had been using was reserved by another family and that we would have to move. Little did we know that there was a $100 fee to rent a cabana, but the gentleman told us that cabana number 14 was available and recorded our room number. We relaxed on the water front for a while, although it seemed like we were both distracted by our phones and staying connected to the outside world. Kaidyn was messaging her friends on Instagram and likely other social media sites. I had rid myself of most social media platforms as a New Year's resolution, and fortunately, I have recouped many hours per day on what would otherwise be spent reading and posting to Facebook. However, I took a half hour or so to respond to a series of postings on one of our squadron pilot chat groups on Viber. Comments were being made about a minor occurrence that happened at the weekend's UTA. Several of the pilots had been late to a briefing following our lunch break which earned an unfavorable reaction from the briefing's facilitator. Without getting into the specifics of what happened, I felt the need to weigh in on the matter and promote professionalism within our officer corps on both sides of the discussion. Knowing that I'm now one of the older members of the group, I signed my post "Professor Hooper" for a good measure of humor.

The hotel employee checked on us and asked what we would like to drink. Again, I ordered sparkling water and Kaidyn enjoyed a zero-proof cocktail of some contraption. He informed us that he wasn't sure when the power would be restored but that there would be a limited selection of food available shortly, including hamburgers and hotdogs. Kaidyn called the spa to see if she could book herself an appointment for a massage, and I asked her to book one for me too. Not surprisingly, the spa was booked for the day, but Kaidyn was informed that she would receive a callback if a spot opened up. Sure enough, her phone did ring. One cancellation had happened, so she was offered an appointment for 2:00p. I figured that would work out perfectly. When she was finished at 3:00p, we would drive south along Honoapiilani Highway toward the Maalaea Harbor near the U.S. Coast Guard station in the valley. We were scheduled for a sunset luau dinner cruise from 5:30p – 7:30p with the Pride of Maui. Knowing that traffic can frequently be heavy on our way into town, we would leave the hotel with plenty of time to spare. Time permitting, we would drive through historic Lahaina along Front Street and maybe make a stop or two along the way.

I knew that Kaidyn would not want to go to her massage on a full stomach, so we would try and eat lunch close to a normal time. The hotel had set up a grill outside the Starbucks. They had a limited menu—hamburgers were $26 and hotdogs were $20. Salads were also available along with soft drinks and bottled water. The credit card machines were still down, so only room charges were being accepted. The employees were taking orders on slips of paper that they would hand to the cook. The line to order wasn't particularly long, but there must have been many scores of people who had ordered their food before we did because it seemed like a very long wait. The line of people waiting to order grew significantly after us. I was unable to hear them calling out names very well, so I inquired a few times on the status of our food. I didn't have any shoes on, so as the pavement was heating up, it was a little painful to walk between the seats we had found and the order stand. By the time our hamburgers were ready, we had waited over an hour and a half for them. At this point we were just thrilled to be able to eat something, and we chose to eat close to the building in the shade so that we wouldn't risk having our food carried away by the wind that was still very strong. After we were finished, we went back to the room so that Kaidyn could get ready for her massage. When she left for the spa, I proceeded to read three more chapters for my master's class. Ironically, the book is called 'Hazard Analysis Techniques for System Safety' and addresses subjects such as safety risk management.

Kaidyn returned to the room around 3:00p as expected, and we prepared for our departure to the dinner cruise. When we left the hotel at 3:42p, it was very windy. A large tree had fallen onto the eastbound lane of Kaanapali Parkway. Cars were on the roads though and we followed the citizen-generated detour along the westbound lanes of Kaanapali Parkway. While proceeding south down Honoapiilani Highway toward Lahaina, I noted that the power lines seemed to be 'wobbling' on their poles and even mentioned to Kaidyn that those power lines could give way. We could see an area of smoke emanating from an area east of town that did not appear to be affecting the roadway or town at this point. However, from what I now know about the timeline of events, a fire that had burned earlier Tuesday morning had been declared to be 100% contained. The flames reignited at approximately 3:30p, flaring up and accelerating toward the town at an exceptionally rapid rate.

We made it as far as Leialli Parkway, just south of the Civic Center, the fire station, and the U.S. Post Office. The situation was changing very quickly and the police set up a blockade. We were the second or third car that was ordered to turn around and head away from Lahaina. There has been a lot said in the weeks following the fires about the questionable performance of the authorities during the crisis. I agree that they have a great deal to answer for. Why weren't the sirens going off, and why didn't our phones blow up with text messages telling everyone to stay away from Lahaina? That being said, from what I know about what was to hit Lahaina in a matter of minutes, we may owe our lives to that officer who sprang into action to seal off traffic that was heading directly into danger. Unfortunately, I'll never know his name.

The excitement for us was only beginning. We were now proceeding northbound along the side of the road that contains the high-power transmission lines. Within a matter of seconds and a quarter of a mile from where we had turned around immediately to the north of a small road that leads to the Lahaina Civic Center, the wind picked up to a howl—up to 60 mph by some estimates. The utility lines snapped and collapsed upon our rental car—a grey Nissan Maxima sedan—at 3:59pm. Kaidyn let out a short scream, and I rapidly braked the car to a stop. It was one section that seemed to only impact our car, and—to a lesser extent—a pickup truck that was largely spared the direct impact. There was a cable directly on top of the car and other cables on both sides. The right-hand mirror was broken off and there was minor damage to the top and sides of the vehicle. We were uninjured and there were no sparks or fire.

Once that happened, I knew it was important to stay in the car absent a greater threat. We had no way of knowing whether the power lines were energized. Numerous passersby in the opposite lanes were taking photos or videos of us on their phones. One of them shouted to us that we needed to get out of our car, but I did not sense any imminent danger that would have necessitated us to act quickly. The best thing would be to stay calm and in the safety of the car so that we would not be directly exposed to the threat of electrocution. I called 911 at 4:02p and provided our location, type of vehicle and license plate, and situation as best as I could. I must have had a poor cell phone signal because the other side of the conversation was intermittent, and then the dispatcher was asking me the same questions over and over again.

I decided to hang up and try texting 911 which actually worked quite well. I wrote, "we are trapped under high power transmission lines....stuck in car (Nissan maxima)....on roadway....high power transmission lines fell on top of car and we can't go anywhere". She needed a more specific location, and I was able to pull up my phone's map and try and identify nearby landmarks. "We are on highway 30, not too far away from the post office....south of Hyatt Regency, north of Wayside Park.....need police/fire dept assistance". The dispatcher told me "just stay in your vehicle....there is a lot going on in Lahaina right now so they will get to you as soon as possible". I just asked her to make sure the power was shut off, and she said they would check on it. I didn't know it at the time, but we actually were quite literally right next to the Lahaina fire station and the police department. But, like she said, they were all fighting fires.

We probably waited under the power lines for a half hour or more. During this time, I received an email that our dinner cruise was cancelled due to weather. Kaidyn texted her mom to let her know that we were trapped under powerlines. Eventually, a good Samaritan approached our car from Kaidyn's side. We rolled down the window and I called out to the man that he may want to get away from these power lines. I'm not sure who he was, but he was dressed in street clothes. He told us that the power lines were cold and had been since 7:00am, and he pointed out which ones were the telephone lines and which ones supplied power to this side of the island. The man suggested a way we could back ourselves onto the small road that leads to the civic center and said he could guide us. He told us there was a crisis in Lahaina and the police probably wouldn't be here to help until 2:00a.

The gentleman sounded like he was a local and maybe knew what he was talking about, so I entertained the thought. I still told Kaidyn that I couldn't believe this guy was out here walking around the powerlines and that he was "braver than I". Nevertheless, he had not been electrocuted, so I rationalized this meant the status of the cables were, in fact, deenergized. I left the car running assuming that if we needed to move the car quickly, it would be easier to avoid having to start it up again. He stood behind the car and marshalled us backwards onto the side street and away from the powerlines—we were free! I shook his hand and thanked him for his help, but I will also never know the man's name or what happened to him that day.

     We drove up the winding road into a parking lot next to the Lahaina District Court. I was able to text 911 to inform them that a good Samaritan helped us get free of the power lines and that their assistance was no longer needed. The dispatcher thanked me for letting them know, asked about the status of the car, and gave me a phone number that I could use to file a police report for the damage the following day. Cell phone service on West Maui didn't last much longer, and Kaidyn was unable to update her mom that we were okay until much later. I wasn't sure how to get to where I was going—or even for sure where I was going—at this point. I made a left turn down a small road parallel to the highway that ran in front of some tennis courts to Leialii Parkway where the police had set up the blockade to prevent vehicles from driving towards Lahaina. At 4:44p, we could see billowing black smoke that had taken a far different form than what we had seen just an hour prior. Almost everything south of this location, including the grass in front of us, was completely destroyed by the wildfires.

     Kaidyn and I proceeded on Honoapiilani Highway toward the hotel, driving past the still downed powerlines that blocked the northbound lanes. We arrived at the Marriott at 4:50p and returned to our room. While she decided to relax for a while, I went back to the car in the garage to see if I could reattach the mirror and buff out the scratches that were on top of the car. The mirror was detached but dangling along the right side of the Nissan. I was able to place it back in position, but it would not have stayed there on its own without using special tools. The scratches were largely superficial and I was able to buff most of them out, but there remained a few minor dents. My next thought was to call Hertz and my insurance company to report the damage, but by now phone service was no longer available.

The car was drivable, but we would have to leave the right-hand window down and keep the mirror inside the car so that it would not continually smash against the side of the car and risk being lost.

It is important to understand that we still had no idea of the scope of the disaster that was unfolding in front of us. We were still planning a drive to Hana on the east side of the island on the following day. The question in my mind was whether or not to return the car to the airport first, face the music for the damage, and try and pick up a different car for the rest of the trip. This mindset might seem ridiculous when looking back on it, but we were still thinking in terms of some high winds and a few wildfires that would come under control soon and maybe the power would even come back on by the evening. Sure, the smoke was bad but I certainly wasn't contemplating a massive loss of life, a city in complete ruins, and a full-blown crisis worthy of national attention. What we found was that we tended to be the last people to know what was really happening. With no electricity, no wi-fi, and no cell phone service, the outside world was receiving far more information than we were.

At the Marriott Ocean Club, guests were on the beach......swimming, surfing, relaxing in the chairs, etc. Restaurants were unable to cook, and the hotel ran out of propane to even grill burgers. We understood that we wouldn't be eating anything until they got the power back on. Some people, including myself, were staring at the plume of smoke that was blowing over the city. The wind carried the smoke out to sea where it encountered a dramatic lifting force over the warm waters as if to grow into a dark towering cumulus cloud.

As the sun set around 7:00p, signs of flames from Lahaina became clearly visible, as seen in these photos taken at 7:18p and 7:51p, although even here I thought I was looking at a handful of individual fires. Obviously, there would be some significant damage, but I still didn't see it for what it was—that the whole city was being mowed to the ground before my eyes.

Chapter 5

I WOKE UP on Wednesday morning around 5:00am. Kaidyn was still sleeping, so I walked toward the beach believing that the overnight hours had provided an opportunity to extinguish or control the fires from the previous evening. What I saw looked like World War III in progress, like Armageddon, and thought this must be what hell looks like. I envisioned what a city might look like if bombs were dropped from directly overhead, and this was it. The fires were not controlled; they were much, much worse. While it seems ridiculous knowing the story in retrospect, I think it was the first time I thought that this was "really bad". I didn't know how bad as I was about three miles away. That's not far, but it's not right up close where one can accurately assess the destruction. The damage would be bad, but certainly the people would have evacuated long before their homes were engulfed--right? First reports were that six people had died. That's bad enough, but it would not be until after I returned home that I learned that Lahaina was completely annihilated and the loss of life could be in the hundreds—maybe 1,000.

Before sunrise, I walked as far south along the beach toward Lahaina as I felt like I safely could without getting in the way. This took me about 2/3 of a mile to Hanakao'o Park that sits at the end of the row of resorts. The fires would reach to within 3/4 of a mile of this location. I was confident that the hotel residents would have been safely evacuated if the fires threatened the hotel directly—as the manager had assured us so. However, the more I think about the way the evacuations were handled from the city, I am not so sure. Where would we have gone anyway? It wasn't until much later after I decompressed from the event and realized it shouldn't be overlooked that we were exceptionally fortunate…very lucky that the flames didn't also take out the hundreds of us guests staying at these resorts too. The fires stayed to our south but not by much, guided by the strong winds that were blowing from the high terrain out to sea.

As I walked back toward the hotel, light began to fill the sky. Cell phones would occasionally grab a signal, probably from the nearby island of Lana'i. I was still unable to access data, although the occasional text message would come through and I even got one or two messages to go out. A small handful of people knew that Kaidyn and I had ventured to Maui and were inquiring as to our status. My Aunt Tutti saw where I was on the Life 360 app and had messaged me. Otherwise, I had kept the trip pretty low key and didn't see the need to sound the alarm with the rest of my family and friends that I was isolated on Maui. We were supposedly safe at the resort, and there wasn't much anybody from the mainland could do for us. I ran into one man who was trying to fly his drone but was unable to successfully takeoff. Not only was it still very windy, perhaps the drone was smart enough to know that flight restrictions were in effect in the area to prevent interference with emergency operations.

Since I had lacked the foresight to stock our room with a few days' worth of bread, peanut butter & jelly, and bottled water when the opportunity had presented itself on Monday evening, my concern turned to sustenance. We had no clue where our next meal was going to come from. I reunited with Kaidyn at the room, and we decided to drive to Whalers Village where they have a shopping center with an ABC store. There was a line of perhaps 50 people waiting for the store to open at the regular time of 8:30am. I got in line and Kaidyn walked to the beach to see if she could obtain a cell phone signal. Opening time came and went, and there was no sign that the ABC store was going to open and no employees in sight.

We walked to the Westin where they appeared to be serving a normal hot meal to their guests. It was clear that the food was for their registered guests only, but we were not staying at the Westin. Later that afternoon, we would see them preparing chicken breasts and a decent food menu for lunch, but again…only for Westin guests. They stated that they were unable to run credit cards, so the only means they had to collect money for the food was through room charges. I recall mentioning to a few strangers that I struck up a conversation with on the beach that in the 'good ole' days, there were these little mechanical devices that you could place a charge slip in and imprint the card manually—there was no need to "run" the credit card! On the other hand, I can appreciate that the Westin knew that food was going to be limited and felt an obligation to take care of their guests first.

Kaidyn and I drove back to the hotel parking garage, and she decided that she wanted to hang out on the beach. We separated at this point because I was still determined to spend as much time as necessary until I found a meal for us for the day. My priority was to make sure that Kaidyn could eat. If I ended up having to 'fast' for a couple of days myself, I think I could manage that, but I wasn't going to let that happen to my cousin if I could help it. I walked to the lobby of the hotel where one employee was handing out granola bars—I grabbed two of them.

I then decided to drive north—solo—to the town of Kaanapali, where I knew there was a Times Supermarket and food truck park. There was a police presence blocking roads to the supermarket. Were they trying to see to it that supplies could be distributed in an orderly fashion, or were they just trying to keep people from looting the place? —I really don't know. I parked next to the food truck park that had been secured by fences. One of the food trucks appeared to be serving food, but two people at a time were being escorted from the fence to the truck. There appeared to be a line of a hundred people or more to access this area. To scope out the situation further, I drove north along Lower Honoapiilani Road. Most of the businesses were closed, and those that were open had lengthy lines waiting to get in. One particular shopping center only had a snow cone shop opened, and there appeared to be a lengthy wait to get in. At least from the car I was able to tune into a radio station that was putting out information about the emergency response—up to this point there had been no information provided.

After a sufficient joyride through Kaanapali, I decided I might fare better with a meal to just go back to the Marriott to see if I could ascertain their plan. Nobody had lost their sense of civility in the town yet, but after reading the 2009 novel *One Second After*, I knew it wouldn't take much time without food before society degenerates into chaos or martial law. On the way back, two young men or teenagers were hitchhiking on the side of the road walking toward the hotel. I would ordinarily never pick up people hitchhiking, but in a time of emergency—I felt like we all should pull together. They didn't need to go far—just to the Hyatt Regency—and they showed their thanks by giving me one of their Smuckers peanut butter & jelly sandwiches. Back at the Marriott, the manager described a grim situation. Many of the hotel associates had lost their homes and were sleeping in the hotel's hospitality room. They didn't have any propane to cook anything but were trying to find some. They provided this update:

AS OF Aug 09 0940HR

- FIRE IS NOT CONTAIN

- THE ROADS TO LAHAINA IS CLOSED
  - NO AIRPORT TRAFFIC
- DO NOT GO TO AIRPORT IF YOU
  DO NOT HAVE A CONFRIM RES.

- POLICE DEPARTMENT IS ALLOWING
  TRAFFIC GOING NORTH IF YOU HAVE
  A CONFIRM RES. HOWEVER THESE
  ROADS ARE DANGEROUS TO DRIVE
  ON

- HAWAIIAN ELEC. STILL ASSETING
  THE SITUATION. ANTICIPATED
  POWER TO BE RESTORED
  LATER ON TONIGHT.

There was a long line of people forming in the lobby in front of a table. Hotel employees were serving a choice between a small salad or a bowl of ramen noodles—one per guest. I walked to the back of that line that was perhaps 200 people deep and waited for over an hour for two bowls of noodles. By now, I had spent half the day to find enough food to last us for possibly the rest of our stay in West Maui. I took what I had up to the room, but Kaidyn was out and about and I really had no way to get ahold of her. The noodles were warm, so I decided to go ahead and eat my bowl and find Kaidyn afterwards. They were delicious, but when food is scarce, I suppose that anything is delicious! I took advantage of the opportunity to fill all of the containers, coffee maker, etc., with drinkable water while we still could. There was no telling how much longer the water would be safe to drink or if the faucets would even operate at all. The hot water was already gone, so if you wanted a shower, it would be a cold one.

I walked back out to the beach and found Kaidyn. We commandeered one of the cabanas; this time nobody was collecting rent from us. I gave Kaidyn the granola bars and told her I would go upstairs to get the rest of the food. I brought down her bowl of ramen noodles, still warm, and gave her the Smuckers sandwich. She didn't eat all of the ramen noodles, so she must have had enough to eat. I then returned what was left over to the warm refrigerator.

    With survival needs taken care of for the time being, we spent some more time on the ocean front. Kaidyn's phone seemed to be working better than mine, so I asked her to send a text message to my mom to let her know our situation and back up the text messages that I tried to send to both of my parents. She was able to touch base with her mom that morning, which was a good thing. The last her mom had heard, she was trapped under power lines. There was still no access to email or internet and no electricity. We played in the ocean for a while, although I had enough after about 15 minutes of battling the strong undercurrent.

I decided to walk south along the beach to Hanakao'o Park again. It was about 2:45p when I observed numerous helicopters dropping buckets of water on the fires which appeared to have subsided a bit. I considered that good news for Lahaina, but I fear the fires started to die out because there was little left to burn.

I'm sure that I told Kaidyn at some point on Wednesday that this wasn't exactly what I had in mind when planning a vacation to the Hawaiian Islands. I said that I was open to trying it again some other time if she was, although I was determined to do my best to salvage whatever fun was left, even if it just meant hanging out at the beach until we figured out what was next. I have a hard time believing we would have been able to take this picture of us enjoying the peaceful ocean shortly after sunset on Wednesday if we had really comprehended the true level of loss of life and property that had just taken place so close to us.

Chapter 6

THURSDAY MORNING BROUGHT another early wakeup. One small fire was visible at 5:45am, but otherwise it was under control. The winds had died down as well, and Hurricane Dora that had passed several hundred miles south of the islands was moving further to the west.

While cell phone service was still very spotty, it was now possible to access internet data and additional messages were beginning to ping to my phone. I emailed my professor to inform him that I would do my best to get my homework in when due that evening but that I may not have the internet connectivity to get it submitted on time. An email came in to inform me that our snorkeling tour that was scheduled for Thursday morning was cancelled due to the ongoing emergency. I wasn't expecting anything different, but I had been concerned that I was unable to cancel the $459.46 excursion and might be held financially responsible for it—perhaps the ultimate 'first world' problem.

I ventured to the lobby to obtain an update on the situation and to look for a place to charge my phone. There was a small generator running that had power strips plugged in. Some of them had additional power strips plugged into them, which is probably not the recommended setup. I managed to find a place to plug my phone in since it was completely dead. News from hotel management was that we were initiating a mass exodus to the Kahului airport. Beginning at 9:00am, busses would begin shuttling guests to the airport where there were special flights set up to evacuate the tourists to Honolulu for $19 per seat. From there, the Federal Emergency Management Agency (FEMA) would assist us in finding onward flights back to the mainland or lodging on Oahu.

I asked the front desk clerk how this would work, given that we had a rental car. She stated that they wanted us to abandon the rental car at the hotel and that the companies would come pick up the vehicles at a later time. This was not being presented as a 'mandatory' evacuation, so I would discuss options with Kaidyn. Meal tickets were being handed out from 7:00am – 8:00am, redeemable for a bowl of oatmeal, edamame & two shrimp skewers or a chicken fajita. While Kaidyn was still sleeping in the room, I stood in line and picked up two tickets for the shrimp skewers that would be ready for us at 11:00am.

I let Kaidyn sleep in as long as she wanted to. Around 8:00am, she came out of her room after I had packed up all of my stuff to be prepared to leave. I told her that guests were able to board busses and take a one-way trip to the airport. I mentioned that it could be an all-day event since I didn't know how long it would take to get to the airport nor how long it would take to get on an airplane once we got there. Moreover, I also had no idea if there were rooms available on Oahu or if there were any flights available to take us back to the mainland once we got there. Alternatively, we could wait another day at the hotel since we had a confirmed flight for Saturday to take us to California and then Texas. We might avoid the mad rush by staying where we knew it was relatively comfortable until the backlog of people thinned out. However, there was no reliable estimate for when electricity would return and no guarantee of continued food or water availability. I told her to make the choice. She decided she wanted to take the risk and see what the day had in store by joining the evacuation.

While Kaidyn took a few minutes to get ready, I walked down to the rental car to make sure we had left nothing inside. I also wrote a brief note to Hertz to explain the damage to the vehicle. I went to the front desk to turn in the car keys and then returned to the room to find Kaidyn ready to go. We walked to the front desk with our luggage to check out, and the front desk clerk directed us to where we would need to go to catch the buses. I picked up my phone from the charger, and we walked toward the Hyatt Regency at 9:00am where there was already a long line forming. After standing in that line for approximately 45 minutes, we were being redirected to Whaler's Village. Once we arrived there, a man directed us to the back of another long line, informing everyone that people had been waiting since 6:00am for the busses.

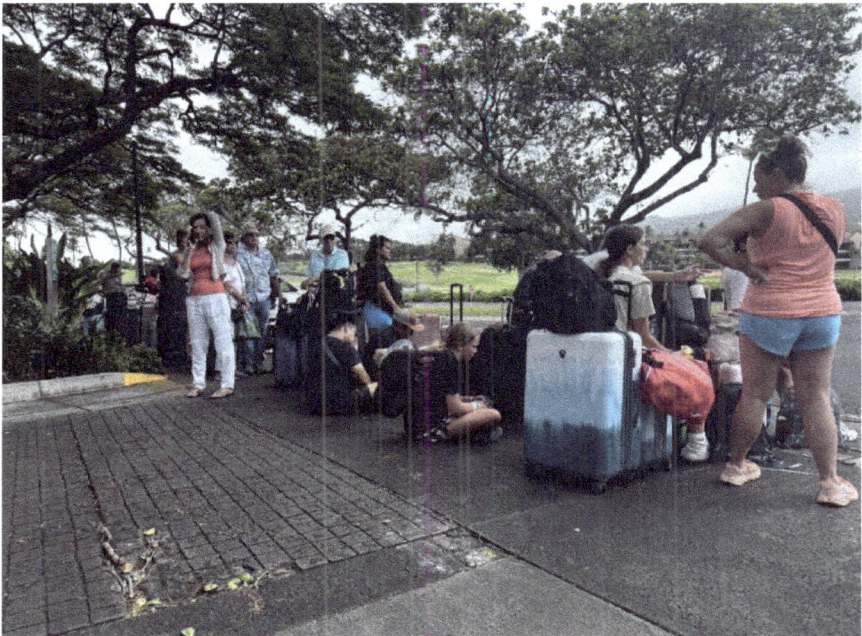

After another hour and a half or so of standing in that line with no busses in sight, there started to be a police presence. Someone on a bullhorn who looked like an authority of some kind announced that those with access to rental cars could get through the police barricade at Lahaina and drive to the airport. They said to drive directly through and not stop to take pictures. We decided that we would check the rental car back out and proceed into town ourselves. Kaidyn held our place in line while I retrieved the car.

The hotel staff that was handing keys back to the guests told us that we were "listening to rumors" if we believed that we could take our rental cars through town. A guest explained that it was a manager standing over there by the police who was making that announcement. He had also said that they had no idea when the busses would show up and thus preferred that we take our rental cars. That made enough sense--why tie up bus space when we can just as easily take our own cars to the airport?

I pulled up to the line where Kaidyn was standing next to a police car, and she made her way over to the car with her bags. A mother and daughter asked if we would take them as well. She was a former flight attendant, and they had been separated from her husband who had been stuck on the other side of the island. I told her that I had three seats but probably not enough room for all of the bags. We threw the backpacks up front with Kaidyn and one of their bags in the back seat with our guests and we made everything fit. Soon, we were on our way in a long line of traffic heading for a police checkpoint just to our south along Honoapiilani Highway.

We slowly moved toward the checkpoint while Kaidyn played her tunes on the car's Bluetooth connection. It appeared that some people were being allowed past the checkpoint into Lahaina and others were being turned away. What would the story need to be for us to obtain access to this road, I thought? After about an hour waiting in this line and observing three large school busses and three more large tour busses drive towards the hotel, we finally reached the police checkpoint. I explained that we were evacuating to the airport in our rental car and that we had been told we could come this way. The officer told us that only local residents with ID and busses were being allowed past the checkpoint.

He stated that our only option for driving to the airport would be the hazardous north route by which we had come into West Maui on Monday afternoon. That was not my preferred course of action because if there is a mass evacuation down that road, there is only one lane. I asked the officer if that was recommended, and he stated that it's not a great road even on a good day—which I already knew. If one car breaks down, runs out of gas, or if anything happens over there, then there is really nowhere else to go. However, that road was open and they were letting us go that way. The only other choice would have been to return the car back to the hotel and get in line for the busses again which would take an undermined amount of time. Nobody was receiving cell phone coverage, so there really was no one to call to obtain accurate information. While not ideal, we made the decision to evacuate to Kahului northbound through Kahakuloa.

The first few miles of the drive saw lighter traffic than I was expecting, although eventually we reached the back of a line of cars. For some reason, traffic was still being allowed into West Maui from Kahului. Several areas of one-lane road required outbound traffic to yield to inbound traffic and we would have to share the roadway. It would have made more sense to restrict inbound traffic for a few hours to allow the evacuation to proceed unhindered. However, there were zero police or authorities on site. Private citizens were directing traffic and managing the flow of people into and out of West Maui. Extreme care had to be taken to avoid clipping the car against the rocks on the right side of the road while also avoiding some of the pickup trucks that were coming the opposite direction down the single-lane road. I jokingly said that we were already missing the right-hand mirror, so it wouldn't be a piece of the car that we could mess up again. The views were beautiful, and I snapped a few pictures along the way.

A shirtless man on foot approached our car and wanted us to stop so that a logjam of inbound traffic could move. I was prepared to honor his request, but my guests in the back of the car seemed uncomfortable with the situation and were screaming for me to 'go'. Perhaps they thought the guy was going to try and rob us—I don't really know, but I took it at face value that they had perceived a danger that I wasn't picking up on. I proceeded around him along the road as did a few other vehicles behind me who were unwilling to stop. It felt like a jackass move on my part as we all had limited roadway to share and were perhaps making the logjam worse. However, I felt obligated to look out for the safety of my three passengers, even if it was only their mental safety. This was also the 'wild, wild west' and nobody had put these fake traffic cops in charge. There should have been officials managing the situation. At a minimum, they should have orchestrated a unidirectional evacuation.

Chapter 7

THE REST OF the drive into town proceeded drama free. As we approached Waihee-Waiehu, cell phone service started to resume—sporadically at first but then more steadily. The mom, whose name escapes me, was able to establish contact with her husband so that we could determine a meeting place. He told her of a national guard checkpoint that we would encounter at the base of Highway 340, although no such checkpoint was found to be in operation. It was agreed that we would meet in a parking lot next to a food truck. Sure enough, she spotted her husband's vehicle in the parking lot and we pulled up alongside. It was an emotional family reunion, and Kaidyn and I were happy to be able to rejoin them together. This was perhaps the happiest part of this story. While our guests had moved along, we were starving for some 'real' food. We decided to stop at the food truck and order ourselves a couple of loco mocos with sprite. Kaidyn also ordered herself a pineapple, and I ordered a chocolate fudge desert. It was the best meal ever! Since it was the first time we had a real cell phone connection for at least two days, we were able to catch up on outside communications.

One email had arrived from United Airlines stating that our flight the next day to San Francisco was cancelled and that we had been rebooked for a flight leaving Saturday afternoon. I looked to see if there were any hotel rooms on this side of Maui where we could stay while awaiting our new flight. If we could find one, we could perhaps forego the need to fly to Oahu. Unfortunately, I was unable to find anything including an Airbnb accommodation. We made our way to a gas station near the airport so that we could refuel the rental car and then proceeded to the Hertz turn-in lane. I explained to the check-in clerk that we had some damage to report and told her what happened. She had me fill out an incident report, and to date that is the last I've heard about it. We caught the train to the terminal where I assumed that I would see where all the evacuees were gathered to wait for flights. There didn't appear to be any organization, so I asked an employee what the process was for getting to Oahu. The worker told me that I should check with Hawaiian Airlines and directed me to the check-in line.

Kaidyn got in the long line with all the bags while I decided to go talk to United Airlines and see if they had any way to get us back home ASAP. I got in the premiere line since we were booked in first class. Without asking me what I needed help with, a United agent told me she was going to help the people standing behind me since they were running late for their flight. After what seemed like half an hour of standing in this line, I was told to go to a different line for rebooking. By then, Kaidyn told me that she had reached the front of her line at Hawaiian Airlines and was wondering what to do. I told her to just let people go in front of her until I returned. I walked to a different line to be helped by United, and it turned out that it was also the wrong line to be standing in. There were no signs that would inform us of that fact, but after standing in that line for a while, an agent pointed me to yet another line for 'rebooking'. I asked her how I was supposed to know where the rebooking line was, and she told me that's why she was there to inform us—after I had been standing around for 45 minutes or longer.

At any rate, when an agent called me over to her counter—which was right in front of the first premiere line I had been standing in—the agent told me that no more flights to the mainland were available that day. Knowing that I would need to go to Oahu since there were no other places to stay on Maui except for the airport or in a shelter, I asked her to find us a flight out of Honolulu. She rebooked us on a flight from Honolulu to Los Angeles, then Houston, and finally home to San Antonio—departing midafternoon on Sunday, August 13.

While I was waiting for help, I looked online for Hawaiian Airlines flights to Oahu. I happened to find them for sale for $19 each one-way; therefore, there was really no need to stand in line. I grabbed those $19 seats right away because I knew they could sell out at any time. Next, even while I was waiting for an answer from United on whether we could get to the mainland tonight or not, I locked in rooms at the Ohana East hotel in Waikiki Beach, Oahu. Kaidyn told me she wanted to check her bag because she had items that would not be let through security. We proceeded to a check-in kiosk where I attempted to get the $25 bag check fee waived as a military member. The kiosk directed us to see an agent to waive the fee, but no agents were readily available to help us. I went ahead and paid the fee so that we could be done with it, and then Kaidyn took her bag to the drop so that we could then proceed to TSA.

The line to security was surprisingly short and we got through in just a few minutes. I had neglected to remove a water bottle and sunscreen from one of my bags so they were confiscated. They also spent several minutes going through my backpack, looking through all of the electronics that I had in there. Once we were airside, we had a couple of hours before we needed to catch our flight. I decided that I would make a call to the Ohana East hotel to verify that we had confirmed rooms that had been booked via Hotwire. The front desk informed me that they had nothing booked for us and that they were completely sold out. I knew that rooms were going to be hard to come by since all of the Maui evacuees were being transported to Oahu, but I thought it was better to find out now than wait until we arrived at the hotel.

I sought out assistance from Hotwire via their texting service, trying to figure out if they could help me book rooms. Moreover, why did they charge my credit card and tell me that we had confirmed rooms reserved when this was not the case? Hotwire stated that they were attempting to find rooms on Oahu for us. They later apologized that "the hotel is unable to honor the reservation" and that everything was sold out--they would be refunding my credit card. I knew we would likely end up sleeping in the convention center with the rest of the FEMA evacuees if we were unable to locate rooms soon. Fortunately, I called the Navy Lodge on Ford Island and they were able to accommodate us on base. With confirmed rooms verified directly with the front desk, I then encountered one of my fellow Delta pilot friends—Walt—who was operating a flight back to Los

Angeles. He had his wife and two kids with him. They were traveling on standby and were unlikely to obtain a seat on the full Airbus 321. He mentioned that their Plan B was to take a flight to Oahu and figure out the rest of their itinerary from there.

Soon it was time to board our Boeing 717 for the 30-minute flight to Honolulu. As we would be staying in the Hawaiian Islands for two days longer than originally planned, Kaidyn and I endeavored to make the best of the remainder of the trip before heading back to Texas. We were able to take an evening fireworks cruise along Waikiki Beach and drive to the North Shore for an hour of horseback riding. We ate in a nice restaurant on top of the Ala Moana hotel, walked through the International Market in Waikiki, and hit up some of the popular tourist attractions like Dole Plantation.

As we prepared to fly home on Sunday, we arrived at the airport to discover that our flight to Los Angeles had been delayed by a couple of hours which would result in missing the connection to Texas. We checked with a United representative at the Daniel K. Inouye International Airport. She informed us that the only other option was a single seat to Denver the following day, which would only take care of one of us. Otherwise, we were stuck with the option to be stranded in Los Angeles overnight. While I had made it an objective of the trip to provide Kaidyn with first class accommodations, I knew that she was trip fatigued and just wanted to go home. I found that Hawaiian Airlines had just one economy class seat left for sale on a nonstop Airbus 330 flight to Austin, Texas leaving that night. If I was going to fly with her, I would have to resort to an airline pilot commuter trick known as 'jump seating'. Basically, that means I would volunteer to ride as an observer in the flight deck with the pilots if all other cabin seats were occupied.

I asked Kaidyn if that was an acceptable plan to her, and she said 'yes'. I booked Kaidyn the last seat on that plane for $1,309.50, and she arranged for her boyfriend Duncan to pick her up in Austin— about a one-hour drive from where I left my car in San Antonio. We had about seven hours before we had to catch the flight to Austin. By this time, Kaidyn had seen all she wanted to of the island, opting to stay at the airport rather than go back into town. We visited the USO lounge in terminal two which provides an area for military personnel and their families to relax while traveling. I used the time to write a paper for my master's class, and Kaidyn was nice enough to edit it for me. Before we knew it, we were leaving the lounge to proceed to terminal one to board the Hawaiian Airlines A330 bound for Austin. It was a redeye flight that arrived in Austin at approximately 7:20am on Monday morning. After collecting our luggage, we were on our way back to San Antonio, assisted by Duncan.

Epilogue

WHILE I KNEW the events in Maui had become a major national headline, it wasn't until after I returned home that I truly learned how devastating the situation really was in Lahaina and how the loss of life was going to reach monumental proportions. While presented from the narrow viewpoint of two tourists visiting the island on vacation, I don't tell our story pretending that we experienced anything close to the horror of those who make Lahaina their home. I feel terrible for the people of Maui. If you are able to donate resources to help them, please do so. You can go to https://www.redcross.org to learn how you can help.

The experience was also a reminder of how much we take the conveniences of modern life for granted. Next time I am faced with a choice on whether to stock up on essentials needed to survive for a few days off-the-grid, I will avail myself of that opportunity—while that choice is still mine to make. Natural and man-made disasters are a reality of the world that we live in, and we must strive to do what we can to always be prepared.

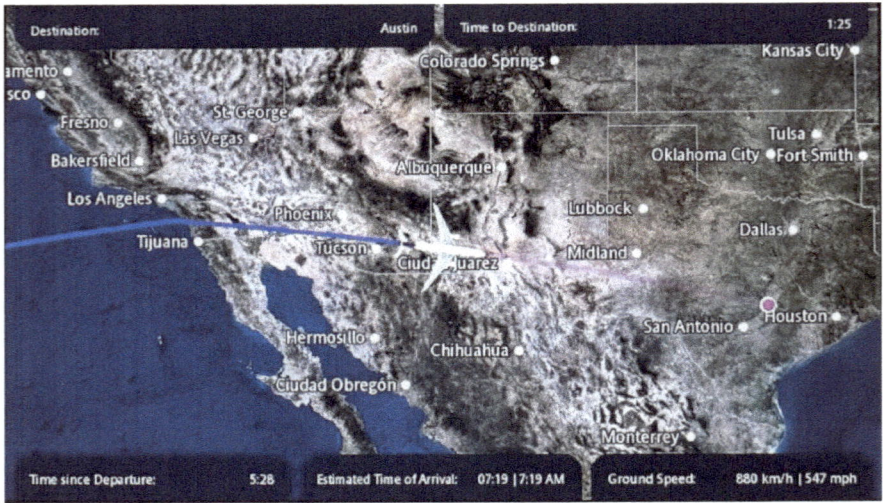

Email: jeremyhooper@yahoo.com

Additional Footage: https://youtu.be/UhAEG54Pdlc?feature=shared

.